The Write – Age Writing Book

The Write-Age Writing Book

The Chrysanthemum Literary Society

Koon Woon

Disclaimer: All persons, names, and places have been changed or invented. There is no legal basis for a lawsuit.

Goldfish Press

Copyright © 2016 by Koon Woon
All rights reserved

Published by
Goldfish Press, Seattle
2012 18th Avenue South
Seattle, Washington 98144

Manufactured in the United States of America

ISBN 9780971160170
Library of Congress Catalog Card Number: 201491859

The Write-Age Writing Book

No matter what is your age, it is the write-age to write. In this workbook you will be presented with prompts that will enable you to start writing. You do not have to follow any particular format or style, genre or length, diction or voice. Just try to be YOU. You are the creator and you are the subject. If you can't be your own boss anywhere, here is where you are the absolute boss!

Please allow me to introduce myself and say more about myself as we progress. Right now I will reveal that I was born in a rural village in China in 1949. Without further ado, here is the first prompt.
Write as little or as much as you want using this prompt as a trigger.

They come at us with hatchets

I had this horrendous nightmare that my father is really a vampire, the lead vampire and I was infected! In the village we attend Party meetings and toil in the rice paddies but when we sleep, our bodies open with a thousand sores, and we need blood to coat our sores. Nowhere is this found in Party Literature and we are forbidden to speak, write or even think of it.

At day, everyone greet us deferentially, but it is only due to the fact that the Party had appointed us, and if they know that we suck their blood with our phantom proboscis while they sleep, they would tear us apart limb by limb.

In the morning everyone wakes with a sense of violation. They have been drained of their blood and robbed of their strength. This is the way we collect "taxes" for the Party, and one may call it the Old-Fashioned Way, the way that cannot be told, but the way that is the way...

My father orderss me never to tell. When by chance his mosquito avatar meets with mine sucking the same victim, he gives me the skull and he takes the thigh. "I get the fat and you get the bone," he says.
I oblige because I am a dutiful son. I help my father planting rice as well as harvesting it in the rice paddies. But we are not fat from rice; we are fat from others' blood. If they know that I am writing this down, the victims and even my father would come at me in the daylight with hatchets.

(Begin writing here)

Next Prompt:

Revenge of the morning glories
"Ever desiring, one sees the manifestations.
"Ever desireless, one sees the mystery."

Mowed down and mowed down again, the overgrown
Adjacent vacant lot of blackberry bramble, daisies, and what
Appears to be parsley and skunk cabbage, unruly grass and morning
Glories – cut, chopped, slashed and mowed…

"Thorns and thistles spring up where the army has marched…"

But this morning, looking out the window, I see the revenge of the morning
Glories, not one but a field of them have come back from the dead, trumpeting
This wild garden

That Schopenhauer would approve of in the Chinese manner –
Like hair of a wild child, and dense to the degree of obstruction
And to catch a body *"coming through the foliage…"*

(Begin responding here)

The black cat

She did not cross my path. I did not see her until I was out of the flowers dense on both sides of the sidewalk. I glanced over to my right on the walkway. The cat was pitch black except those tiger-like green eyes that flashed. She was tense, paranoid, and ready to pounce. She did not. But as Aaron Nimzovitch said, "The threat is more dangerous than its execution."

I felt sad when I realized that this cat had been abused or harmed in some irretrievable way and its origin is lost to history. It is not like some other cats that nuzzle up to you and always get treats and get treated warmly. This cat will always react hostilely to anything that would elicit alarm in the remotest way. And for that behavior, it will be further ignored or mistreated.

(Begin writing here)

Next Prompt:

Crows

I am beginning to like crows and their caws as if a sealed coffin is opening. Petroleum black, their blackness oozes of dangers and filths of the night. Or so imagines one of the polluted sectors of the city we deem to be. The city at night is of opened knives as the surgeon cuts the flesh of a wounded man from too many pleasures in a night club. The ambulance was abrupt, as the man seesaws between life and death; the way to go is not to bleed too profusely.

I am beginning to hear the caballero speaking to his compadre, while bleeding copiously from all his wounds. The old man denies he is anymore himself or that his house is his own, while a Taoist novice in China quotes the Tao Te Ching – "The way that can be told is not the way; the name that can be named is not the name."

An old woman dials the phone. A voice asks, "Do you want a boy or a girl tonight?"

"Let's try a girl this time."

In Morocco the sands are white against the bronze bodies of girls and boys. In China tonight a water-buffalo finally expires from perpetual toils. We are still throwing soda cans into the garbage in our Emerald City Seattle, while the urban forager is one meal from death.

Next Prompt:

[I am going to make it easier this time] The prompt simply is:

I drink sake, the brew of the far yeast

(Begin writing aphorisms and Haiku etc.)

Next Prompt:

Cityscape with Solitary Figure

Not a sparrow is yet up, nor the milk trucks.
Even to malign him, the street lamps are frugal.
He who is under the shadow of the building, a deeper shadow.
He who hauls his house on his back.
Must we avoid acknowledging him?
He whose going does not make an arriving.

In the darkness he is white, brown, or black –
No one can tell or would tell.
He knows the various grids of the city and how far
Into the morning before he can get a free cup of coffee.
The park benches are partitioned
And signs saying no camping. What a life!

Formerly there was shelter from the rain
Beneath the bridge, but the stench of graffiti
Forced him to brightly-lit doorways before dawn.
Merchant-hired security sweeps him
Up in the morning and he goes as a lump
Of coal in the snow, going just for the sake of go.

(Write a socially-constructive poem)

Try your hand at another poem:

Two birds, one tree

Two birds, one tree
Two birds in one tree argue
over its span, its symbolic reach,
the meaning of it all, the seeds,
the fallen leaves,
finalized by gravity.

Two men in one boat discuss
the ripples on water,
the bob and the line,
the murky depths,
in fathoms beneath.

Four creatures thus converse
across the elements of
wind and water,
growth and grossness
of life and its demise.

That the wind may blow
and water perturbates,
that men and birds imitate
the world's inadvertent sounds,
as time is lost and we lose ground
the note and the nodes,
its liveliness casually found.

Try another poem:

The Strength that's Required; the Strength that's Denied

I guitar chord dizzily fellow roomers in the alcove
of a delicious life, when raindrops fall equally
on doorknobs of copper and doorknobs of silver

In the strength that is required and in the strength that is denied,
I have not seen myself in print,
not even in the obituary column

As I find life in the "as is" condition,
my road is not for the feign heart,
as I ask myself if it is the right path

Knowing that I can be a "stepping stone"
or a "stumbling block" of History
that may or may not grant me even reprieve.

Will I music my incompleteness into a syncopated line?
A timeline of sorts when the captain leads his sailors ashore
from a ship with broken mast

When ladies of the harbor bring biscuits and flowers
as the tides ebb and flow anew and ever stronger
in the strength that's required,

And in the strength that's denied no more
 as I beat words together like oars slapping the water
to forge the certainty of a people finally reaching shore.

KoonWoon

(Try another poem, if you want to; otherwise, write anything you want)

Can't ever get tired of poetry. Try another one:

Who they read

The young read the young
The old read the dead
The Madam with the deformed hand reads tea
Leaves.

(Have a ball here, whatever you write!)

KoonWoon

Try writing a vignette?

You are not Albert Yu

You are not Albert Yu. I used to know a Albert Yu. I lived in his rooming house. He had been a pharmaceutical sales rep before he became a student slum lord. I did odd jobs for him in lieu of some rent money. He had two huge dogs called "Happy" and "Lucky." He asked me if my father gambled. He said that he and his father in Hong Kong were not on speaking terms because he bought an expensive suitcase and his father criticized him for it. He said he needed that one with the lock.

He took me to a whore house on Capital Hill. He didn't carry any money with him and he borrowed some from me. I supposed he was afraid that he would blow his wad in a place like that. The cops sounded the siren in the alley and the madam said that's how they make sure that they'd be paid off. She said the "girls" were actually nurses "moonlighting."

That was my first time. Zsa Zsa treated me well. That's was after the madam had given me some orange juice and a "marriage manual" to read. I think the gist of it was "in, out, repeat if necessary."

Years later, another former student tenant named Bruce who drove a metro bus at the time saw me at the HUB. I was mentally ill and homeless and I carried and played a guitar. Bruce asked me if I knew what had happened to Albert. I said no. Bruce told me that Albert had blew his brains out.

I thought Albert was happy. He married a beautiful woman from Honan, China and had driven me to his house to talk one time. He said that Herfy's in the U-District was full of "too many ears." I was paranoid. I said I was being followed. A helicopter buzzed above. He laughed and said, "You are being followed!"

When Bruce told me that he had blew his brains out. I said, "Correction. The CIA got him."

Try another vignette?

The Early Years

The time my father arrived in Aberdeen was 1951. He didn't want his sons grow up to be gang members in SF Chinatown. He had been one and decided he rather chase the American dream in a small town on the West Coast. Hank, his first son in America was born in a taxi on the way to the hospital. That's why Hank was always in a hurry all his life. My father worked for his Uncle Benny at the Canton Café. My dad was the strongest and so he had to stay after closing time to clean the stoves and the grill, while the other cooks were taking a shower. Benny otherwise overworked my dad and my dad had one kind after another for several years. Though my dad complained about his low wages, Benny would say to others, "He's got so many kids hanging onto him like grapes on a vine, where is he going to go?" And so one Christmas they had a dinner party at the café and my dad had to cook all the steaks. Benny picked out the smallest one and gave it to my dad. My father handed it over to the waitress and walked out into the night.

He then worked at Ocean Shores Inn and later at the Smoke Shop Café owned by the Aberdeen Mayor Walt Failor. That's when I arrived from China in 1960. We lived in the Aberdeen housing projects. Then there were 9 of us in a small three-bedroom duplex. Then my dad worked for Sally in Montesano. She was the madam of a whorehouse. I helped my dad with kitchen work at the China Doll Café, the cover for the house of ill repute. The real business was upstairs. I was confused at age 14, and got more confused when the cops started coming in because the girls were in trouble. When the madam was run out of town, she stayed with us at our housing project on Oak Street for a week or two until she came up with the money to pay the sheriff in order to leave town. She claimed to be giving work to troubled girls who could not otherwise find work. And she gave me a tape recorder that was hardly used. Years later I figured out that she was taping and blackmailing her "johns." It was OK to run a clean house of prostitution if she paid off the mayor and the sheriff. But it was not OK to blackmail people. She was always telling me to ask the old lonely men to give me quarters for the juke box on slow Sundays. She told me her favorite fruit was blueberries. I went out to the foothills of the Olympics to pick a pint of it for her and I put it in the walk-in fridge for her. She never ate a single one.

Sally was always saying it is too cold in here or it is too hot in here. My dad tells me she is on too much drugs. After Sally left town, somehow my father got all the restaurant equipment and managed to transport them 10 miles to Aberdeen and started his own little Hong Kong Café right there on Simpson Avenue. He put his sons to work and when we made a go of it, his Uncle Benny finally came to visit us, and my parents cannot show ingratitude and they were solicitous to Benny about his health. I knew what to do though. I brought Benny his cup of obligatory tea. I asked, "Does grandfather Benny need some sugar in his tea?" I knew full well he had diabetes though.

Courtesy of a friend, we will use a play of his for our next write-age write:

KAN FA (PERSPECTIVE)

                        CHARACTERS
                        Professor Whang — noted teacher
                        Mrs Whang — his wife
                        Young Student

SCENE: Seattle Chinatown — International District

> *(Professor Whang, Wife and Student stand near Whang's top floor apartment picture window.)*

STUDENT Professor Whang, I've left my parents in Sacramento as an artist to learn perspective. I've heard that you are a master in the seldom mentioned Song Dynasty technique of horizons, called "Kan Fa".

PROF WHANG Kan Fa! Ah! Very obscure.

STUDENT Yes. That's why I've come to Seattle, to your budget condo in Uwajamaya Village. I wish to learn Kan Fa.

PROF WHANG Fine. If you can name and date first Renaissance Italian practitioner, while standing on left foot.

STUDENT *(standing on left foot)* Filippo Brunelleschi. 1377 to 1446. Come on, Professor; teach me the real stuff.

PROF WHANG Ah! Look to point west between two huge Arenas called "Safeco" and "Century Link" Fields. What point to you see?

STUDENT The vanishing point.

PROF WHANG Wrong! It's the point where the ticket prices become too expensive to afford. The Vanishing Point is where players testify on steroid use.

STUDENT This is deadly stuff. *(bowing)* Please teach me.

PROF WHANG I will teach you if you walk my dog each day to her favorite chestnut tree in Kobe Terrace Park ... and other chores.

STUDENT Your dog is a Lhasa Apso. Can I carry her on rainy days?

PROF WHANG I said "walk". And other chores.

STUDENT *(after pause)* Okay.

PROF WHANG *(aside to Wife)* The boy will work well.
MRS WHANG Get him to take out the laundry.

(One year later)

STUDENT Professor, I've walked your dog to Kobe Park for a year. Now am I ready for Kan Fa?

PROF WHANG Wait until the dog gets bigger.

MRS WHANG Get him to pick up this week's Uwajamaya Bargain Flyer.

(Five years later)

STUDENT Professor Whang, I've taken your dog five years to pee at her favorite Chestnut tree and she hasn't grown any bigger. Lhasa Apsos don't grow. Is it time to teach me Kan Fa?

PROF WHANG Ah! You have seen now that it's not the dog, but the tree that draws you. Trees are Time's Kan Fa. Their bare limbs are a Fourth Dimension Map. Keep observing.

MRS WHANG Tell him to collect the chestnuts this winter.

(Ten years later)

STUDENT Professor, I've been collecting chestnuts for five years and scooping up dog poop for ten years and now I think I'm wasting my time. Are you gong to teach me?

PROF WHANG Ah! Today we go to tree in Kobe Terrace. I will teach you "shortcut"?

STUDENT *(amazed)* A shortcut? I've walked there ten years!

PROF WHANG Shortcut in eyes! Not feet.

STUDENT Binocular disparity?

PROF WHANG Shortcut in perception! Point of view. One slip and you learn nothing. Do you understand me?

STUDENT Sure.

MRS WHANG *(aside to Whang)* You're <u>not</u> going to teach him! If he thinks he's learned Kan Fa, he'll leave us!

PROF WHANG *(aside to Wife)* Relax, Bunnycheeks. I have things under control.

(Short time later. Near Chestnut tree in Kobe Terrace Park.)

PROF WHANG Now, young man, as you gaze out over Elliott Bay toward the majestic Olympic Mountain, name the root of "perception".

STUDENT Uh ... ocular discernment?

PROF WHANG Wrong! Discipline! Discipline and obedience fix the root-in-the-eyes, the perspective, the vanishing point. You must do exactly everything I say.

STUDENT Okay.

PROF WHANG Good. Climb up tree to top branch. Keep gaze fixed on mountains. Go.

(Student climbs up the tree and looks at Olympic Mountains. Sound of small dog barking.)

MRS WHANG *(to Whang)* Do you know what you're doing? Fool! He'll leave!

PROF WHANG Relax, Honeybunch.
 (shouting up to Student) Young man, carefully grab top branch with both hands!! Now hang from branch with hands!!
 (Student hangs from branch.) Young man, let go with left hand!!
 (Student hangs by right hand.) Now let go with right hand!!

MRS WHANG *(smugly)* He won't do it.

PROF WHANG We will see.

(Student lets go of right hand, but instead of falling, he rises and floats off over Safeco Field and Elliot Bay toward Mount Olympus among blue Olympic peaks [atmospheric perspective].)

PROF WHANG He floats over Safeco Field to Olympics, to the blue mountains, to China

MRS WHANG Stupid! He's gone!

PROF WHANG (*smiling*) He was going anyway.

    (*Sound of dog barking fades quickly. Dim out.*)

Note: on black box stages or in a theatre without a fly gallery
the Student on a platform upstage simply mimes the tree climbing,
hanging on branch, and floating off.

Martin Ingerson
Seattle

Prelude:

The following are a series of vignettes or ruminations of my life as lived or imagined that may intersect. Various people or the same characters would pop up here and there with different identities or persuasions with or without my permission or intention in different incidents or events.

I have lived my life now into my 64th year. Reflections in a certain sense are a luxury. I take this good fortune to toy with them, hoping to be emotionally true in some sense, but expecting self-aggrandizement to eat up the truth at times.

What you are to do is to write what seems to be significant, even though isolated memories and reflections in vignette form. Good luck to self-discovery.

Koon Woon

Koon Woon
Seattle
The Canton Girl

Time it was when she said, "Because you cannot real work and I not real college, I am sad, my sad friend."

I had finished tutoring her for the night. She piped water from the wash basin in the corner of the tenement room into a bucket that came from a nearby restaurant. It once held oil or mayonnaise. She sat on a stool and washed her underwear. I sat at the edge of her bed. Her father was in the adjoining tenement room. Malicious people said that she and her father had sex. He is an old man of 80 who reads day-old newspapers. I heard that he had been imprisoned during the Cultural Revolution. I did not think any less of him or his younger daughter, whom I dubbed the Canton Girl. Canton is now called Guangzhou; it is also my native city.

She told me this of the Cultural Revolution, "I was a fat bureaucrat, although I was very young, because my father was an official."

"One time my father became crazy," She continued, "he thought all the radio broadcasts were saying, '"Old Rui, you are a bad man.'"

"My father went to hide. We looked for my father. After a long time, I found my father in a garage. I said to my father, 'Father, it is OK now. You come home.'"

Coming to America, the Canton Girl had worked first as a seamstress and then as a warehouse clerk at an import/export company. Her English was strong enough. She had taken two years of ESL and my tutoring.

I lived in #317 on the same floor. When I came back to my room I sat at my little table and faced a big piece of cardboard with which I shut out the lights of Seattle Chinatown and the Interstate 5 freeway, the thoroughfare from Tijuana, Mexico to Vancouver, British Columbia. To my upper left were a small bookshelf and a clamp-on lamp. My other source of light is the overhead naked bulb. I was revising a poem about the convoluted muscles of the eagle that the deepness of the night and instant Folgers coffee could give my own brain. I was fighting sleep and depression. This chaos was depicted best in a Haiku my best boyhood friend claimed to have written in high school creative writing. It went something like this:

   At the edge of swamp
   Bravely the lone little frog
   Holds back night, croaking…

It was so striking that I remembered it and I told him years later how great it was. He confessed

that he didn't write it. Basho did.

Fortune Telling and Other Supplications

*****

My father doesn't like to talk much. Uncharacteristic of him, my father repeated this story on several occasions after closing hours at our Chinese-American restaurant. We would be sitting on metal milk crates at our makeshift table at the side of the humming walk-in box near the back door. He would have a big steak platter heap full with Texas long grain rice with a one-pound rib steak piled on top. He would pour soy sauce over the steak and some on the rice. He is still in his white shirt with a pack of Marlboros in the pocket. I would join him when I finish cooking a chow har (prawns stir-fried with seasonal garden vegetables). Likewise I would have rice, but only about half the amount. We would eat in silence for a while and after a particular large and satisfying mouthful of steak fat and rice, he would begin.

"I went to a fortuneteller when I was young, and she told me these things," he said quietly and almost conspiratorially, "you are going to have a benefactor (benefactress), many "small persons" will follow you, and the older you get, the better off you are." I nodded in agree

"Sally helped me," he said. He meant that she gave him the restaurant equipment from her defunct restaurant to start his own. I had a very low opinion of Sally and I decided that restaurant work was slavery and so what did she do? She enslaved him and made him in turn enslaved his entire family. It is just like Frederick Engle said, "In a capitalist society, the man sells his children as widgets of labor to the State." When I was young, I considered any "service" job beneath my dignity and it was temporarily enslavement to be gotten out of as soon as possible.

But there is no escaping family, especially a Chinese family steeped in the Confucian filial piety.

A little digression to "Sally" if I may, Daddy O! You may have liked Sally because you may have been a partner in her China Doll Café, a cover for a house of ill repute. But that Sally was an exploiter of human flesh. There were Lee, Ginger, and Suzy in her employ. The bouncer Leroy who also doubled as a cook. That entourage of "mayors," "sheriffs," who craved my boy ass. They got a bar there and it is difficult to know who is drunk and who is the Neal McCoy. Sally would wave to me and say *propina* and I would go and take the sucker's quarter and drop it in the jukebox.

*****

MDR

Sometimes it was in the foothills; sometimes it was in the valley. Mostly I found myself alone at the MDR coffeehouse in North Beach in San Francisco. MDR stood for Minimum Daily Requirement. The barista did not speak to me after making my espresso. I sat near a window and glanced out at the unusually quiet intersection – Columbus and Grant Avenue.

You would think that in the friendly city with the Golden Gate Bridge spanning a long stretch of the San Francisco Bay that I would have a friend or two, a lover or two, or at least someone to play chess with. I don't know whose fault it was. I read, drank, and brooded alone. Weldon Kees' car was found parked near the Golden Gate Bridge and he was never found again. I came to San Francisco with that kind of Donald Justice expectation. What did all this mean? I said it; I said what I said, but it would be years later when fragments would fit together. It was as if a rogue Soviet spy ring stormed the city by a conspiracy perpetrated through an arrangement of the public pay phones.

My family on their way to Disneyland came to see me at the Stockton Hotel. It was on the corner of Stockton and Vallejo, upstairs of a butcher shop. Blood was on the sawdust floor and occasional killing occurred upstairs at the hotel. I was oblivious to all this. My friends kept me supplied with drugs and even showed a letter of a friend in a Turkish prison. Would anyone believe me that I read Sartre and Camus here and played Go against myself? An occasional telephone call to my then girlfriend who ceased to be faithful after a month was a crazy way to resurrect the love. I was on the last of my money, money I saved up from working for the post office. This worried me.

I came with a companion. I drove down the coastal highway with him from Seattle. We drove down the coastal Highway 101. Here is a poem about those years:

Coastal Highway 101, 1960

It was in effect a river of sorts...
The ocean returned its water across vacant hours
at the slow crossings of afternoons in
low-blood-sugared towns while the pale
lights of taverns burned

The barber sat in his chair listening to
the vacuum-tube radio, the cigar
vending machine full of Indian-head
nickels,
the Emerson
Hotel with its
dark stairs
leading to dens
of vacancy

It was in effect a town of sorts...
The ocean lapped its tongue here, mudflats harbored musssels,
loggers shook dice
for schooners of
beer while the sky
threatened rain
all day

Chinese cooks diced string beans a mile long,
their work expanding to fill idle hours, the
Pacific tides contracting and expanding
across the pretense of commerce
when small fishing boats returned with Dungeness crabs 3 for a dollar

It was in effect a time of sorts...

High school
graduates still
stayed in town, and
pulp and paper mills
saturated the air
spelling jobs and a fair shake for small home owners

Those towns were
strung along Highway
101, the scenic route to
Pacifica, California
where surfing was just getting on newsreels
and soda was still dispensed in cold glass bottles

It was in effect a life of sorts,
when Viet Nam was still some unfamiliar place in the Orient
and Ricky Nelson was a traveling man with a
pretty gal in every port and the price was
right every night and Groucho still hit his
marks

Those times and places burned like LSD
flashing and burning into the next century... But basically
it was a time before waking up to the enormous world as it stirred
while the miser still counted his pennies...

A more recent poem, written about the time I was a student at the University of Oregon:

April 11, 2012
She was a strange lady; she said
the truth is calculable but I am so sad.
I was attracted to her false eye,
in the coffeehouse when I read
a philosophy text and vastly enjoyed
my coffee stirred with honey
that being young and impressionable,
I fed copious info to my head.

She studied Chaucer and the cups and saucers
of the busy café and said, "I must go to bed.
I worked on a chemistry problem and I am balancing
the valences in my head."
In the end it was no good.
The chess competition was extremely bad
although the steam from my coffee
held its own for a while
against the fog on the stained-glass window,
and outside, the snow fell. Sort of sad.

She told me of the phone company
where she patched calls
with signals coming from the other side of the world
criss-crossing in her ears.
So many people talking still, she said,
the world must still be undead.

I touched softly her hand and bid to go.
She sighed weakly as gentle as the falling snow.
In the short interlude while I touched her hand,
a lifetime slid by and henceforth
all chance meetings follow this paradigm,
as the global swelling of the earth's tides,
and our parting did not signify a good-bye...

Jose

Jose always leaves a trail of water and bits of vegetables when he works in our restaurant kitchen. In a way he leaves traces of himself where he has traveled and lived. He leaves unfinished business behind. Here is a man who's traveled and lived in three continents only to die in a hotel room.

Not that he didn't have family; he had two simultaneously -- in Hong Kong and in Peru – two wives but none of his children is his biologically, however.

My mother is Jose's sister. The fact that she calls her older brother "Jose" instead of elder brother is a sign of disrespect, and we, her children follow suit. But I always call him older maternal uncle, as he is deserving to be called just because of the order of his birth.

"Take back your wife, Poi's mother," my mother is frequently admonishing, "so that you will have someone to take care of you in old age and burn incense when you *Shang tian*."

"But I did not adopt Poi," protests Jose, "that woman did herself," referring to his legal wife in Hong Kong.

"Too late to argue such matters," my mother cuts curtly, "your Peru woman is a foreign devil. At least your wife in China is Chinese."

To this Jose is without a ready reply. It is not easy for a fifty-year-old man who doesn't understand English to get along in America. He depended on his sister's family for work and psychological support, even though they are largely cruel to his needs and unsympathetic to his poverty. They, having just escaped the housing project in a small town made them acutely aware of the shame that came with poverty.

They can't imagine that Jose might have had such bad luck too.

Gold Glints and Glares

Three sections of gold glint and glare
inside the home of a rich man;
while, a poor man has two vinegars against one oil
and lice under sweaty armpits.

I shop for pen to ink a blameless childhood,
where the pristine currents flow in brooks,
where water gurgle and slip under mossy rocks,
where ferns fan out to call your truant name,
in the woods that enclose you,
in the childhood forest now tucked far, far away.

Take your mansions and haciendas,
take your edifices of glass and steel,
your cities designed by interstate firms,
take your uniformed guards and firearms,
but the city still will fall in the deep night,
when random weeds entropy in,
even as the bureaucratic city council
declares a no-trespass year.

Why does your mood keep deteriorating?
Was that a random remark that went unrecorded?
How can you uncross your arms and swing them
through the languorous air?
How many parking meters are needed to fund
one bureaucratic seat of this emerging city of ours?

The cars loop around; the cars loop around.
Our four television stations vie to televise the baseball game.
Loud music emanates from passing cars,
with windows roll down and each one shouts
Mother of Luck!
How the untamed winds from the shore barge in!

Unkind city, the homeless men are cradling
newspapers, filching for aluminum cans;
they are the hordes of shopping cart soldiers
trying to find targets to vent.
On the ninth day out of the military,
they still have not pulled into shape their identities.

Last seen was the mayor of the city
and an out of town dignitary in a limousine.

Unreal city, through a psychotic haze,
women look fat in furs, and when the summer wind
drives away the late snow, out come the derelicts
to huddle in the park,
as the ship comes in with another load of illegal immigrants.
Phoneless in an SRO, footsteps echoing
sleeplessness down the communal hall,
recalling the writing of fantasies in a coffeehouse
and slamming poetry on Wednesday nights.
Unreal city, unkind city, and three coins in the fountain
is advance payment for a cup of coffee?

Mr. Schuler and the Triple-L

"Do you need help with going to the bathroom?" he asked.

"No," I answered. This was the first of a series of questions that I didn't feel like replying to, as it was cold and austere in his office.

"Do you have any dietary restrictions?"

I didn't like the word "restrictions" and so I said "No." The snow was drifting down outside the window. I had lug my suitcase from the road to this compound because the taxi couldn't drive in the unshoveled snow. It was a bad year in Seattle. The worst snow in 20 years. But the hospital paid for the cab.

"You know," Mr. Schuler peered over his steel-rimmed glasses, "Mr. Woon, I think you are a smart man. You can think your way through troubles, and so I don't think you will be here too long."

The space heaters made a clicking sound. The heater was trying to come on, but it rather sounded like Morse or military codes. And Mr. Schuler was not a literary figure but a former colonel in the Air Force.

"Do you have a will?"

I did not answer. Such a question is not culturally-sensitive.

"Do you have a will?"

He asked again. His had suddenly looked very large.

"I am very tired," I feigned in a weak voice. Can we do this interview at a later time. Now I do need to go to the bathroom.

"You will do just fine here. I am thinking of putting you to work here. Being part of the scheme of things will make you feel more at home here." He then "volunteered" me to help the breakfast cook to wash dishes.

"You won't be here very long," he repeated. He picked up the phone, and a few minutes later Andy came and led me to my cottage.

I saw three beds in my room, one of the three rooms in the cottage. I peered into another room where the television sound bites were coming from. I saw three motley men sitting at the edge of their beds, each watching to a separate tv. I thought, "Oh shit, here is where I am going to be, waiting for Godot."

But then I remember what the Colonel had said, "You won't be here very long."

I saw that in the alcove there was a little table with a jigsaw puzzle in progress.

I sat there for a moment. I looked out the window. I was in my winter jacket and the cottage was unheated. The snow was drifting down. It was 4 pm or so, but it was already getting dark and the white snowflakes drifts and drifts down, and some of them landed in the crotch of a birch tree.

I realized finally I was at the Triple L. I was not in a hurry to meet my fellow residents. I took out my journal. This was going to be a serious writers' retreat.

This is not the Triple-L.

women are building latrines and you got all the time in the world?

They confiscated his deck of cards.
They said,"Women are building latrines. Everyone is reconstructing our socialism. And you got time to gamble?"
His wife was having a baby, a boy, but they didn't let him go home. They put him in jail.
He said that it was an addiction, an illness.
They said that he did it because he was addicted to his own adrenalin, a way to get high. But it was so expensive. Every gambler loses sooner or later.

So he was in the stench of his cell.

The Voice of America was broadcasting.
In Seattle three guys robbed a gambling joint, hogtied 14 and shot them in the head and only one survived. But it was the Tao that he lived to testified and put them all in prison. They said that it was simple robbery.

Looks like 2 guys won't ever get out of prison but the third man is up for parole. The public is out to convict him; they let the public to decide? Vigilante justice? Denial is not a river in Egypt, Tipping is not a city in China and Regret is not a bird.

You figure this one out.

It was an exclusive club. I never been there. Didn't even hear about it until the worst massacre happened in the history of Seattle hit the radio and newspapers. And it split or galvanized the Chinese community.

I don't even buy a lottery ticket. The last one I bought was a legal one from the State of Washington back in 1984. Here is the mathematics of it. I give the State $1.00. The State says "Thank you." Then it gives me back 42 cents. Well, that is the odds of real, regulated, and legal gambling. You don't have to be a genius to figure out the odds of "controlled" gambling. Welcome to the club, they say.

There was a time I bet on which fly takes off from the table first. I was that addicted. Then horses. The only horse I like now is Elmer's glue. Them sons of bitches told me it was "sport of kings."

You get lucky and bang big ding dong.

If you got that much time and energy, why don't you help the women build the latrines that are sorely needed in this town. You can't piss for less than 50 cents.

(see attached mug shots)

mug shots. "have a cup of tea, Uncle."

Kurt Vonnegut Jr. wrote that in America, there is money to be made like you can just scoop water from a river. The trick is that if someone would tell you where. When my Dad was working at the China Doll, I was his kitchen side-kick. But dimmit to hell, the upstairs was a whorehouse. When the madam paid me a dollar an hour for working into the wee hours of the weekends, I bought a tape recorder. My Mom beamed that I spent money on something technological. She told my Dad, "It is good that he is learning to like money." And then she asked my Dad, "What do they charge for a trick at the place? Ten bucks?"

Years later I read a book about the backstretch of a racetrack. They refer to a ten dollar bill as a sawbuck. Those goofy jockeys come to eat at my cousin's restaurant in Sausalito, California on the house, and tip my cousin Nelson which horse was going to win in the ninth race at the Bay Meadows the next day. They never get in a sweatbox to shed weight. All the info on the racing was wrong, full of misprints. They just say to Nelson, "Bet on Wales tomorrow in the 9th, he hadn't won for a while." They took care of each other. At your expense.

KoonWoon

A "Woman of the Dunes"

Venus, Venus Fly Trap
He who enters prepare to lose all hope
Sad songs love there sleeping
Time arrests it, and when freed, time has also flown.

I quit playing poker when I felt guilt winning all the marbles that we wager. I lost that competitive edge and after years of drifting, living on the edge.

Lady Luck was my bedfellow although she rarely gave out sex. But Diane would anytime.
Keller said that when he fucked her, her rolls of belly fat hang and drooped over her cunt.

"Hard to find it," Keller laments. "And you," he says, "it is unbelievable you got that impotence problem, your mind is so sensual; I mean sexy."

Keller would ingest anything, legal or illegal, and he needed Quaaludes to sleep. He described his psychiatrist as an Amazon-like woman. "She can toss me into the river, or otherwise eat me alive," he contended. But somehow he can coax her to prescribe pretty heavily for him.

Keller, though a mess, did not or will not lose his competitive edge, he described the walking from Jackson Heights to Chinatown as a game of football, dodging everything and everyone along the way, and he was not kind enough to refrain from criticizing the odors in Chinatown.

I would get even with Keller. Besides having Iris sit on my lap all the time in the third floor kitchen, I would fondle her small and firm breasts. Keller is green with envy and protests to Iris.

"And what's wrong with me?" he protests to Iris.

Iris' father used to dress her in tights and take her to parties where she plays the guitar and sing. Her favorite song was "500 Miles."

Iris's reply to Keller is always the same, "I would always lose something to you, Keller, if I even let you touch my lips, let alone enter."

Iris's last name was Gaton. She spoke with a French accent. She spent her childhood in France. She explained that she was catatonic one time and they brought her to the hospital. Iris admired me for being able to do inorganic chemistry. I did my homework with a pitcher of ice water and a pack of cigarettes. The fact that people sat and talked at the same kitchen table with me didn't distract me. I was that focused, but I would just as easily lose it to free-floating anxiety.

Her eyes are accustomed to see in the dimly lit flat on Grant Avenue. Especially dark was the piranha fish tank that she partially covered with cardboard. My Fat Aunt would scream at me whenever she spied a roach. I then swoop that pest up and throw it in the tank. The piranha shoots up from the lower depths of the dark tank and tears that roach up and as quickly, it would dart back down to the tank's bottom after this hasty meal. She did have a good setup I have to admit for killing two birds with one stone.

She shouts at me when she wants me to watch television with her in the evening, otherwise I would stay in the bedroom reading library books. I didn't just then know how lonely she was. Her son Martin was shot to death in a gang related incident; which I knew later was related to a drugstore robbery. She had called my dad and my dad had called me while I was in Seattle. I was deciding whether I should take a math test for this Native girl so that she would become the first token female American native to receive a degree in science. She told me that Dr. Kingston, the undergraduate advisor for the math department was her friend and would rub my back.

"I need you to come home," my dad ordered.

"But I got to finish my math degree."

"This is a matter of urgency. Your cousin Martin died and she needs your company. She called me and she wants you to go down to Frisco."

"Why, what's wrong, Barbar?"

"Get on the Greyhound, and when you get home we will discuss it."

My dad's impatience alerted me to some sort of uneasy premonition. I told the girl I didn't want to take the test. She offered me money. Maybe if she offered sex I would have done it. But she had a blue eyed blond boyfriend that drives a jeep. An ex-marine he was. I said the hell with her, she didn't have any native pride. Angelina I am not going to pry you from being a token.

My heart was wounded and my knee was hurting. I came directly home to Aberdeen.

Sometimes…

Sometimes rooming house quarrels over the communal table,
Where Joe leans his bicycle, Frank about to eat his mushrooms.

Sometimes voices out in the hall, so a door is a pretense,
The world comes into the pallor of my room.

Sometimes things grown in isolation compensate with exotic a;
People fear and at the same time admire a fancy tomb.

Sometimes internal voices drive us across the ridiculous
To Nietzsche's abyss and up Wagnerian heights to doom.

Sometimes when the sheriff comes to inquire about my thoughts,
I exhibit recent advances in Calculus I computed in my room.

Sometimes he'd smile custodially and say,"My place is not where you want to be,
And so don't be writing critical verse, nor set off 'crackers that go "Boom!"

Kaya Memoir [September 3, 2014]

There isn't that much to scrutinize about my life. I am narcissistic. My father, a fry cook for the mayor's smoke shop café in a small town, scolded me, when I wanted to wear contact lenses because many high school kids were sporting them.

 "Who the hell do you think I am, and who the hell do you think you are, even President Johnson wears glasses!"

But I went to the optometrist anyway and tried contacts. The optometrist put them onto my eyeballs with his fat fingers. I sat for an hour. The lenses burnt like hell and my eyes watered.

"You are too sensitive," the optometrist said. That was before soft plastic lenses. Long before "plastic" was the "one word" in the movie "The Graduate."

I took Contemporary World Problems from Mr. Ron Langhand. Mr. Langhand allowed us to quote verbatim from the textbook, which was mainly a compilation of all the wars since the Great War. And he allowed us to do our homework in class. Mr. Ron Langhand had played college football. He wasn't real big, but he was solid with convoluted muscles in his arms and neck that we can see. He had a standing challenge to the boys in the class to arm wrestle him. The challenger can declare a win if he last more than a count of ten from an observer of the contest. Mr. Ron Langhand said he would give an "A" to anyone who can last ten full seconds.

Kendall Wilson was the only guy who took up the challenge. I had delivered the Oregonian newspaper for his father Mr. Wilson, but I never learned his first name. Mr. Wilson is a tall, thin man and he is quick on his feet. He told us he shadow boxes at home. Kendall used to come with us when we sold newspaper subscriptions door to door. He seemed to be sleepy or depressed all the time. Mr. Wilson drove us in his four-door Ford sedan. We would split up and I would carry several copies of the day's paper under my left armpit. Typically a woman of my mother's age or younger would answer the door. She wouldn't be wearing a negligee despite what William Carlos Williams told you. No, she would be properly dressed in pants and sweater, having just dropped her kids at the elementary school. I was told to step right up to her and to thrust a copy of the newspaper into her hand and say, "Mam, I would like to present you a copy of today's award-winning newspaper. They never ask what is the award for. It has complete news about local, national, and world events for your husband, not to mention the financial page and you might even find a bargain in the wanted ads. The coupons in the paper would be enough to recover what your subscription costs. And it is delivered to your house six or seven days a week. There are lots of comics for the kids. And it is being offered today at a special rate. You can save 50% over the regular subscription price of
$1.30 for daily delivery except Sunday, and Sunday is just $1.00 but we will take off ten cents if you get both the daily and the Sunday for $2.20. Now the papers is selling 10 cents a copy on the stands, so you actually save over $2 a month if you get both the daily and the Sunday. You could help me out a great deal because I am trying to win a trip to Janzen Beach with my brothers.

That's when we were kids around the ages from twelve to sixteen, all morning delivery boys of the Oregonian newspaper. In six short years, Kendall grew into some kind of street kid, although that was before the time of official street kids, but there was marijuana in the schools of bigger cities. Kendall had worked up and he had strong biceps. He lasted about six seconds against Langhands. Langhands said, "You did OK, so I will give you a "B" for this class. Arm wrestling was considered a "contemporary world problem" and so since Kendall was brave enough to take up the challenge and lasted an entire six seconds, he was rewarded for his understanding of the world situation. None of us was going to argue with Mr. Langhands for a better grade, because none of the rest of us can pin Mr. Langhands in arm wrestling and likely we wouldn't last more than four seconds as in "Fee Fi Fo Fum."

I remember reading Carl G. Jung's book <u>Man and His Symbols</u> in Mr. Ackerland's Study Hall class during idle moments. Mr. Ackerland come up the isle and looked to his left at me and shook his head and smiled, "Who are you trying to impress, Woon?" But it was nearly 40 years before I really understood what a "symbol" was. A symbol is not just a word or a design, but it was a real thing! A military tank is a symbol of a soldier's penis and a nuclear bomb is a symbol of ultimate brute force. And $E = mc2$ is the symbol of ultimate knowledge? Mr. Know-it-all? I know Einstein did not think that way of himself. But a symbol is mistaken for the real thing or worse, we forget about the real thing behind the symbol, and there lies the danger.

Koon Woon
Posted on **December 6, 2012**

"A Season in Hell"

"When you come in to work each morning,
remove your bodily organs and limbs
one by one. Hang them up on the hooks provided in
the walk-in box, then put a white apron
onto your disembodied self, pick up a knife,
and go to the meat block," said Alex the manager.

I was also drained of blood and other vital bodily fluids.

After the morning rush preparing pork adobo and chicken curry, I
ate lunch with Fong the chief cook and Lee the dishwasher.

In the afternoon, I examined souls and kept their merits and demerits in a ledger.

For the three months I worked at City Lunch near the Bart Station,
I paid my rent and gradually became robust enough to walk to work.
The entire city of San Francisco swung with the rhythm of my walk,
and stars appeared in the middle of the afternoon with a sliver of the moon.

Meanwhile, at Fisherman's Wharf, the stingrays came to the jetty
and whipped their tails against rocks; tourists paid me to dance on
the waves. I carefully tread water and remembered to breathe.

In the end, I was evicted anyway from my castle that glowed at night.
For lack of anything better to do, I walked from hilltop to hilltop,
burned newspapers to inhale the smoke, then climbed down to the water
beneath the Golden Gate Bridge and harvested seaweed.

I waited until one sunny day when the water was warm and calm,
then swam all the way to Asia and got replacements for my disembodied self.
I did not forget that I was a ghost. And
that was my first season in Hell.

[September 4, 2014] Kitchen of the China Star Café. Uncle Harry, visibly excited, pointed out to Hank and I, who were just 10 and 12 at the time, the headline on the Aberdeen Daily World newspaper: China explodes first atomic bomb. "We are catching up," he exclaimed, "we won't be the sick man of Asia forever!" My father was less sanguine, he did not say anything about that, but he told Hank and me to peel a sack of onions in the storeroom. This is what I did not like. Hank is faster than I am and he liked to make a race out of it. I feel anger and humiliation to be beaten by my younger brother.

At home we overhear our father say to our mom about his cousin, Uncle Harry. "Bail him out of jail again. Always drink until he is a puke on the street."

"You can't blame him. He got no family here. He go back to hotel room and look at the four walls like a crazy man."

"He accuses us taking all the profit. Your children are white and fat, He say."

"He don't mean it. Maybe he is envious. But you got kids soon grow up to help you."

My father was mollified. My mom goes back to sewing a shirt from scratch. She had worked as a seamstress for my aunt Gim Gee in San Francisco. Immigrants like to sew up three industries – food, clothing, and housing. These are things everyone needs everyday. Not even sex is needed so often. But once you got the basics down, you can entice people to the vices and launder money into the restaurants, sweatshops, and real estate. Chinese are big on gambling.

[Sept 14, 2014]

Somewhere near the pasture town of El Vira, Oregon, the Greyhound bus veered off the two-lane country road, crashed through the wooden fence, careened on two wheels before it landed on its side. The driver had suffered a heart attack. The twenty or so passengers crawled out of the bus slowly, not taking any of the overhead luggage with them. I was the last one to get out of the bus, because I had wakened from a deep-stupor. I had just finished my finals week as an undergraduate student in mathematics and I had a huge sleep-debt. It took me a while to orient myself. Everyone seemed to suddenly disappear as if through a wormhole in space. I started walking in a daze and gradually I recovered my sense of self, but the grassy pasture gave way to soggier and soggier footing, and finally after about 100 or so feet, it turned into a field of rice paddies. I was walking in water-covered mud.

Kaya memoir 2 (1)

Flowers gone

Bees too

Leaves have fallen

Autumn half over

This is where I begin again, knowing the wistful air, my shortened breath. I flit a bit more as an errant bird. Perchance we will hold hands now and walk that far, when snow falls, on my sparse hair. And you will finally appreciate crows, what they know. I don't know that much of the seasons. Except that there are four.

 We have faced the rumbling of oblivion, the erasure's call. No one can teach us now. We must hope that along with mistakes, a bit of luck would fall.

Fifty years ago, we lived in a tenement in that lovely city and received letters from our friends in a Turkish prison, doing time mainly for youthful follies. The trains do not run at midnight in that country. Letters stopped coming. Meanwhile we drank espresso in North Beach. And I scored Galois cigarettes. It is a spelling error. I do not know French. Nor would I ever go to Paris and sit at a sidewalk café and tune my poetry as I would a guitar.

A village boy from China, I boated half-way around the world. School opened up libraries for me. I am one story among the many my father was too busy to tell. He had been the captain of the San Francisco Chinatown valleyball team. My older cousin Benson told us when visiting our town Aberdeen, and before returning to San Francisco, he gave his BB gun to my brother Hank. Then Benson joined the Air Force and learned to shoot an automatic rifle. Then, America was relatively at peace, he pulled weeds at Golden Gate Park; he was a gardener for the City. He was the oldest of eight siblings and soon enough they all had children. My aunt was their mother and she operated two sweat shops that employed a total of 80 illiterate women that are inarticulate money machines. She wanted to open a third. License was denied. Benson went to a hearing in the city council, and he shouted these very words: "Jesus Christ, we are just trying to make a living!"

We lived in the Stockton where Crazy Annie shouted at people from her second-floor window. My friends were on welfare and their tenement room was a depot in the Hippie underground railroad that somehow always managed to have drugs of some kind. A friend of theirs was convinced he can fly off the Golden Gate Bridge and go directly to Heaven like Icarus. He went down into the water instead and was so relaxed when he hit the Bay water only his legs broke, thus dubiously becoming the first jumper to survive the Golden Gate. That's because he had already given all his worldly possessions away. Saint Peter will not take you if you are a welfare case in Heaven.

However Deep the Night I Expect Morning

Fog rolls into the valley, rolls
Where my mind goes into the evening,
As the rhythm of city syncopates my walk,
The roar of jets, the whisper of beggars,
Parks have their statues

In this city I know
Know where to find the best soup,
Where often the bands play the pigeons flock
Above heads of idols and unknown heroes
Not far from my tenement above Stockton and Vallejo;
I play Go from a book.

Rinds of light and rain fall silently
Equally on door knobs of silver or copper
This town dreams are altered by Andy and Val
Fight domestic while mice noisily cum
They do not expect morning

I think of crimson electric when morning sun rises
Arriving like a Chagall painting
A man floats up to kiss a woman from the Bolshoi Ballet

I am writing to you as I do, ever so remorseful
The window sill announces there is rain outside
But your purring has begun here in pulses of 8 to 80
As you break night once more and again
I write to you as I do and writing as you yourself do

On onion skin the lightest of verse
The lightest of verse, the lightest of verse

My most, if I could say it, haunting experience is seeing the public execution of a landlord. That took place near my village in China around 1954, when over a thousand miles away from my county in Guangdong Province, Toishan, the Korean War was raging. Only one man in our village "volunteered" to fight at the front. There were mostly feeble men in our village named Nan-on, which translated as "South Peace." Only one man besides the soldier, was of good specimen. He was my friend Gan Way's father, whom I called younger uncle because I had mistaken him to be younger than my father. My grandmother is the one who tells me about my father.

If my father had committed a crime, arrest him. I am only the son, the one that never shines in social company and will keep his mouth shut because I know nothing. And when I blab, it is my schizoaffective illness that is having diarrhea of the mouth

Thankful for the Movement

Notwithstanding the clear, the warm sun
My footfall dully and dutifully duds the cement.

Impenetrable is reality with a mud façade.

My ennui suddenly ruptured by a handful of sparrows
Camouflaged in the grass taking flight

Joined by more sparrows out the maple trees, diverging...

The movements of birds dissolve the sludge of my existence
As I learn these modes and states

That are like "the plastic parts of poems"

Giving me a bundle of enlightenment
Apart from colonies or hives

To the open road. I am thankful for the movement.

KoonWoon

Endnote: *Koon Woon is a member of the secretive 47-stroke club. These are anonymous writers of China who dare to criticize the emperor.*

Notes:

www.ingramcontent.com/pod-product-compliance
Lightning Source LLC
Chambersburg PA
CBHW051703040426
42446CB00009B/1272